Original title:
In the Light of the Tropics

Copyright © 2025 Creative Arts Management OÜ
All rights reserved.

Author: Harris Montgomery
ISBN HARDBACK: 978-1-80581-687-4
ISBN PAPERBACK: 978-1-80581-214-2
ISBN EBOOK: 978-1-80581-687-4

Where the Horizon Meets the Sun

The sun's a giant pancake, flipped in the sky,
It sizzles and sparkles, oh me, oh my!
Palm trees do the cha-cha, swaying with glee,
While seagulls caw secrets, just for me!

Jewel Tones of the Tropic Seas

The ocean's a jester, with waves made of blue,
It tickles your toes, saying, "Come play too!"
Coral reefs giggle, dressed in bright attire,
While fish throw a party, dancing in choir.

Embracing the Warmth of Coral Islands

The sand is a blanket, soft underfoot,
Shells whisper jokes, with a sweet little toot.
Coconuts tumble down, plopping with cheer,
And monkeys play tag, swinging without fear.

Sun-Touched Dreams of Eden

Bananas play peek-a-boo, up in their trees,
While lizards wear shades, sunbathing with ease.
Laughter's a mango, ripe for the bite,
As day turns to dusk, a warm, silly sight.

The Floral Symphony of a Set Sun

Petals tangle in a swirl,
Dancing with the evening's pearl.
Bees wear shades, buzzing with flair,
As flowers gossip without a care.

Laughter blooms in colors bright,
Tulips sing and tease tonight.
Sunsets play on nature's stage,
While daisies flip through a magazine page.

Sunlight Through the Tropic Veil

Coconuts wear little hats,
Palm trees sway and chat like brats.
Lemons laugh while oranges roll,
Sunlight tickles each fruit's soul.

Crabs don sunglasses, strut with style,
While sandcastles smirk and pile.
Chasing rays on a sandy spree,
They wave goodbye, then all agree.

Reverberations of a Tropical Sunset

A parrot jokes, 'Get your own perch!'
While iguanas plan a sunbathing search.
The horizon blushes, feeling shy,
As flamingos strike a pose nearby.

With laughter echoing over the bay,
Seashells giggle at night's ballet.
Stars appear, like winks from above,
While the moon joins in with a little love.

Daydreaming Under the Warmth of the Sun

Turtles nap in a lazy line,
Under rays that taste like wine.
Squirrels take a coffee break,
While sunbeams start to dance and shake.

Wishing wells toss coins with glee,
As shadows play pretend at sea.
With laughter dripping from the sky,
The daydreams flutter, never shy.

Melodies of Sun and Sea

Seagulls dance with salty flair,
Crabs wear hats, a beachside pair.
The sun's a fryer on our backs,
While dolphins joke with silly quacks.

Umbrellas flip like little boats,
With drinks that sing in funny notes.
Sandy toes and tulip drinks,
We laugh until the whole world blinks.

Reflections on Silver Sands

Mirrors shimmer, oh what fun,
Shells do cartwheels in the sun.
Here comes a kid with jelly beans,
Sandy pockets, sticky dreams.

Turtles giggle as they race,
Waves join in, a splashy chase.
Sunburned noses, shades all wrong,
We hum a tune and sing along.

Celebrating the Hue of Daydreams

Paintbrush skies in colors bright,
Rabbits bounce, a funny sight.
Coconut drinks in silly hats,
A parade of dancing cats.

We toast to clouds that look like cake,
With every sip, our laughter quake.
The sun winks with a playful breeze,
While we giggle under the trees.

Blooming Under a Radiant Sky

Flowers bloom and stretch for glee,
A parrot spills its jokes to me.
Sunshine tickles grass so green,
Nature laughs, it's quite the scene.

Silly hats and flip-flop shows,
The sun can rival even prose.
A butterfly joins our dance,
In this vibrant, wacky romance.

The Pulse of Saltwater and Sand

Waves tickle toes on sunlit shore,
Seagulls squawk, demanding more.
Buckets and spades in a playful fight,
Sandcastle kingdoms take flight at night.

We caught a crab, it waved hello,
Then scuttled away, put on a show.
Laughter echoes, splashes abound,
As the ocean dances, joy is found.

Harvesting the Heat of Day

Under the sun, our faces glow,
Braving the heat, we steal the show.
Lemonade stands and ice cream cones,
Sticky fingers, happy groans.

Flip-flops flying, a comical race,
Tanned legs tangled in a sun-kissed embrace.
The BBQ sizzles with zest and cheer,
As friends gather near, the fun is clear.

Clouds Like Cotton Candy

Puffy clouds drift, oh what a sight,
A pinkish hue turning day into night.
We lay on grass, counting sheep,
While sunbeams tickle, pulling us deep.

Ice cream cones spill, we laugh, we shout,
As sugar rush rides take us about.
Imagination soars up high,
Like those fluffy wonders in the sky.

Sunlit Pathways of Adventure

Bikes whirring down sunlit lanes,
Where laughter echoes, joy remains.
Sandy toes and tangled hair,
Adventures spin in warm, sweet air.

We dodge the waves, like ninjas skilled,
Falling face-first, completely thrilled.
With treasure maps drawn in the dirt,
Every day's a quest, despite the hurt.

A Tapestry of Sunbeams

Sunlight dances on the floor,
While my sandwich calls for more.
A parrot squawks a joke or two,
The local cat just steals my shoe.

Palm trees sway with a bright grin,
Sipping coconut, I wear a fin.
The toucan laughs at my bad tan,
As I splash in with my best plan.

Spices in the Warmth of Sunrise

The rooster crows with morning cheer,
While ants parade like pioneers.
My curry's hot, it makes me sweat,
I grin and wave at my pet ferret.

Mangoes tumble, juice a cascade,
I slip and slide, oh, the escapade!
Beneath the sun, I chase my friend,
Only to trip, but that's not the end.

Beneath the Palms, Life Awaits

Beneath the palms, I start to snooze,
A crab tiptoes off with my shoes.
The iguana spouts funny tales,
While I dream of sailing gales.

With rum punch swaying in my hand,
I dance like I'm in a rock band.
The sun sets low, it winks at me,
As I try to catch a buzzing bee.

Whispers of the Tropical Twilight

The fireflies blink and play around,
While I trip over the ground!
A turtle chuckles at my spree,
As I search for my lost key.

Laughter bubbles, the stars gleam bright,
Who knew a crab could dance at night?
The moon laughs at my goofy stance,
And I join in this tropical dance.

The Dance of Light Among Greenery

Bright beams dapple through the leaves,
As lizards strut in suave reprieves.
A parrot twirls, a feathered dance,
While monkeys laugh at squirrels' prance.

Flip-flops flop on sandy shores,
As tourists try to dodge sea roars.
With coconut drinks, we cheer and sip,
While sunburned noses take a trip.

Tropical Tranquility

A hammock sways between two palms,
Where breezes play like nature's psalms.
Cockatoos gossip, oh what a tale,
While beach balls bounce without fail.

Sunbathers pose, but oh, what a sight!
Sunscreen applied with all their might.
The sand's a comedy, full of slips,
As they tumble with their snack-filled lips.

A Medley of Sunshine and Harmony

Waves crash lightly, laughter roars,
Beachcombers search for shiny shores.
Seashells squeak in the tidal play,
As crabs march in their funky way.

Dancing shadows at sunset's call,
With flip-flops flying, oh what a fall!
Seagulls squawk their silly song,
As we all join in—this can't be wrong!

Garden of Dreams Under Shimmering Skies

Blossoms blush in vivid hues,
As gardeners boast of their best views.
Bees buzz wildly, don't they know?
They're flirting hard, stealing the show.

A toucan's laugh echoes through the lane,
While sleepy turtles forget the gain.
With watering cans, we dance about,
Mixing mud with cheers—what a rout!

Lush Vibrations of the Tropics

Palm trees dance to the beat,
A monkey steals a snack, oh what a treat!
Swaying coconuts join the fun,
Laughing sun shines bright for everyone.

Bamboo stands with a cheeky grin,
While parrots gossip about the din.
Breezes carry tunes that sway,
As flip-flops stumble on the way!

Shimmering Waters

Waves giggle as they kiss the shore,
Fish in shades that leave you wanting more.
A crab in a tux struts along the sand,
While dolphins dance away on command.

Beach balls bounce in laughter's wake,
A sunburned tourist takes a risk and shakes.
Splashing friends with a playful cheer,
What a way to spend a sunny year!

Vibrant Skies

Colors swirl with a playful dash,
Butterflies frolic in a vibrant splash.
Clouds wear hats, floating carefree,
As laughter echoes from every tree.

Rainbows giggle at a cat's sly pounce,
While a toucan's jokes make laughter bounce.
Stars wink down on the vibrant show,
As night paints smiles with a glittering glow.

A Symphony of Tropical Colors

Paintbrushes dipped in playful hues,
Every shade tells a tale that's new.
Fruits wear costumes of wild delight,
While flowers gossip under the moonlight.

A parrot quips with flair and sass,
As the hibiscus blushes, what a class!
Cacti join the fiesta in line,
With cactus jokes that tickle and shine.

Secrets of the Sun-Kissed Jungle

Under leaves thick with laughter and cheer,
Bears tell stories that all can hear.
Frogs croak jokes, wild and loud,
Amidst the warm sun they gather proud.

Lemurs giggle as they swing,
Spinning tales of the wildest fling.
All in the jungle, mysteries unfold,
Sun-kissed secrets, funny and bold!

The Serenade of Radiant Flora

In the garden, plants dance with cheer,
Laughter floats on the breeze, oh dear!
A parrot sings tunes, so full of glee,
While monkeys swing by, so wild and free.

Sunflowers gossip, they can't hold back,
Whispering secrets, in yellow, they lack.
Daisies join in with a chuckle or two,
While roses blush red with laughter anew.

Frangipani smiles, a fragrant delight,
Tickling the noses as they flutter in flight.
Even the cacti join in on the fun,
Winking with spikes, basking in the sun.

As night falls gently, the stars take their cue,
The flowers keep laughing beneath the moondew.
In this funny garden, joy flows like a stream,
A vibrant oasis, wrapped in a dream.

Illuminated Echoes of a Tropical Dawn

The sun peeks up, a jester so bright,
Tickling the treetops, igniting the night.
A sloth yawns wide, stretching slow and long,
As the trees hum along in a quirky song.

Birds are drumming with wings in the breeze,
Syncopated rhythms that aim to please.
A toucan spills juice, what a clumsy act,
While a parakeet shouts, 'Now that's a fact!'

The grasshoppers join with their silly hop,
In a madcap parade, they just can't stop.
Fluttering butterflies, with colors so bold,
Whispering jokes that are never quite told.

As dew gives way to the gold of the day,
Laughter erupts in a melodious way.
For in every moment, under skies grand,
The echoes of joy fill this tropical land.

Sunlit Pathways Through the Canopy

Beneath the green arch, a squirrel gets lost,
Chasing its tail, it's the funniest cost!
Lizards on branches, sunbathing in style,
Giggling away with a lizardy smile.

Vines stretch and twist, a dance of delight,
Wrap around trunks, like a playful sight.
The sunlight giggles as shadows take flight,
Playing hide and seek until fall of night.

A cheeky iguana struts down the lane,
With a swagger so bold, it's hard to contain.
Fungi in patches, so purple and green,
Chime in with laughter, a comedic scene.

As rays filter through, painting all around,
Nature's own circus, alive with a sound.
In this canopy wonder, smiles overflow,
Joy spills from each leaf, where wild creatures go.

Tropical Serendipity

In a land where the sun often shines,
Strange little creatures break all the lines.
A flamingo slips in a puddle so wide,
But gets up with flair, oh, what a ride!

Butterflies flutter with giggles and grace,
Flapping their wings at a comical pace.
An alligator grins, with teeth on display,
Hoping to charm, but scaring away!

The palm trees sway, their leaves start to clap,
Gossiping whispers wrapped in a flap.
What funny events do these days unfold?
A tapestry woven with laughter untold.

As dusk wraps the day, colorful yet bright,
The moon winks down, joining in on the light.
Serendipity twirls with each joyous spin,
In this tropical realm, where the fun never ends.

Embraced by the Warmth of Nature's Heart

The sun sat down with a sizzle and grin,
Palm trees giggled as breezes rush in.
A crab wore a hat, quite fancy and bright,
He danced in the sand, what a curious sight.

Coconuts laughing, they roll and they bounce,
Like jokesters at sea, they laugh and they flounce.
A toucan with flair croaked a terribly joke,
And monkeys swung low, with a playful poke.

The waves whispered secrets, both silly and sweet,
While sunbathers slipped on their own little feet.
One tripped on a beach ball, fell into a dish,
And landed in snacks, oh, what a fine wish!

As fireflies sparkled, they'd dance in the air,
Laughter erupted, no worries or cares.
With tunes of the land playing soft through the night,
The world felt alive, under stars oh so bright.

Harmony in the Hues of Twilight

Twilight painted the sky with a brush of delight,
As parrots mimicked with a comical bite.
A gecko, quite dapper, slipped into a twirl,
While crickets chirped songs — a spontaneous whirl!

A turtle on yoga found balance and grace,
And fish in the sea played a game of base chase.
The moon peeked shyly, a wink in its glow,
While waves rolled in gently, putting on a show.

As stars blinked awake, a raccoon took care,
To steal a few fruits from a party laid bare.
He slipped on a banana, did the brave flight,
And landed face-first — oh, a comical sight!

The laughter spread wide when the sun bid adieu,
Embracing the night with a whimsical hue.
A serenade offered from crickets, what fun,
As nature conspired for joy to be spun.

Reflections of Sun-drenched Vistas

Sunny spots glimmered, the children did race,
Making sandcastles (with a mollusk embrace).
Lizards in shades lounged on rocks, looking grand,
Pretending they ruled, oh, this sun-baked land!

A seagull was plotting some grub to swipe,
While tourists snapped photos; they'd better take type.
One posed with a crab, who thought it was fun,
Until it pinched gently, oh what a run!

The breeze sang a ballad, a tune full of cheer,
As surfboards dipped under salt-kissed veneer.
A dolphin jumped high, with a splash as its throne,
While kids squeaked in joy, and not one felt alone.

Reflections of laughter danced on the bay,
As sunset announced the close of the day.
And in each cheeky wave, laughter would ride,
With sun-drenched vistas that no one could hide.

Tranquil Seas Under a Tinted Sky

The ocean was calm, but the gulls had a shout,
As picnic baskets beckoned, and ants came about.
With sandwiches missing, the scene turned quite bleak,
While kids chased around, becoming quite cheek!

Flip-flops flew off when a wave gave a shove,
And beach balls bounced wildly like kittens in love.
A sandcastle king, all regal and proud,
Waved to a clownfish, who bowed to the crowd.

As sun melted slowly, a twist of delight,
The sky turned to sorbet, a whimsical sight.
A parrot at sunset squawked jokes, oh so slick,
While sunbathers giggled at each little trick.

The tide danced back playfully, pulling the day,
As laughter floated, where children would play.
With treasures of giggles, memories flowed,
As tranquil seas treasured the joy that they sowed.

While the Sun Melts into the Sea

The sun dips low, it takes a dive,
Beneath the waves, the fish arrive.
Seagulls laugh, in a silly dance,
While sunburnt folks lose their pants.

Palm trees sway, with a cheeky grin,
As crabs in tuxedos waddle in.
Tickled toes in warm sand glow,
While ice cream drips—what a show!

Sunset paints the skies with cheer,
Even the coconuts drink cold beer.
Kids chase waves, their joy unleashed,
While beach balls bounce, a sandy feast!

In this tale of a sunny spree,
Laughter echoes, wild and free.
As evening whispers glowing dreams,
The warmth of laughter easily seems.

Tales from the Sun-Baked Earth

In the heat, old sandals sway,
While lizards sunbathe all day.
The humor blooms like vibrant flowers,
As sunbaked folks talk for hours.

Sweaty brows, a glorious sight,
Who knew sunscreen could spark a fight?
Watermelon seeds fly with flair,
As they land in someone's hair.

A dance-off starts near the grill,
With hot dogs flying, thrills to spill.
Ice cubes tinkle in punch bowls bright,
A slip on spills brings pure delight.

Tales of calamity told with glee,
Each twist and turn adds to the spree.
As shadows stretch, and laughter roars,
The sun-baked earth shares so much more.

Drifting Dreams of Paradise

Clouds drift by, like boats in the sky,
While vacationers aim for a pie.
Sipping drinks with umbrellas bright,
A seagull snatches—what a fright!

Tanned tourists here, with big wide grins,
Armed with sunscreen, thick as wins.
Flip-flops flapping along the shore,
They trip on glances and crabs galore!

Rays sparkle like disco lights,
As beach games turn into epic fights.
A beach towel towel war erupts,
And laughter flies, it never interrupts.

As night descends with stars aglow,
They gather 'round with tales to show.
Dreams drift softly on ocean waves,
In this paradise, mischief saves.

Lush Gardens Under a Blue Sky

Flowers bloom with colors bright,
While gardeners dance with pure delight.
The sun's so hot, it makes them sweat,
Yet they pretend it's just a bet.

Bees buzz around like tiny planes,
While kids run wild in sun-kissed lanes.
A picnic spread, oh what a spread!
But ants declare it's theirs instead!

With veggies tumbling from a stand,
They laugh and chase them across the land.
Oh, how the laughter fills the air,
As nature's bounty leads to a dare!

Under the sky, so vast and free,
Life's a garden, a funny spree.
With every giggle, every smile,
The lushness thrives all the while.

Golden Canopies

Underneath the golden hue,
Monkeys wear their favorite shoe.
Tropic hats with colors bright,
Dance around in sheer delight.

Parrots squawk a witty word,
As the locals watch, disturbed.
Coconuts drop, the crowd they tease,
Laughter echoes through the trees.

Splashing water, crabs on parade,
Trying hard to dodge the shade.
Sunburned noses start to glow,
While sun hats ask, 'Where'd you go?'

Even iguanas wear a grin,
In this land where fun begins.
To be a lizard in the sun,
Is surely the best kind of fun!

Sun-Kissed Shores

Sandy toes and missing surf,
Home to laughter, not much turf.
Seagulls stealing fries galore,
While ice cream melts upon the shore.

Beach balls bouncing, dogs will race,
Sticky hands all over the place.
Fishermen fight the ocean's tease,
Saying, 'No bites, just a breeze!'

Sandcastles with moats so grand,
Get washed away by the tide's hand.
Kids run screaming back to Mom,
As the waves come rolling on.

Sunset paints the sky so fine,
While flip-flops often misalign.
Counting shells, we can't ignore,
Life is better at this shore!

Whispering Palms

Palms sway with a sassy dance,
Hoping for a coconut chance.
Sneaky monkeys steal a stare,
Waving leaves, they seem to care.

Umbrellas bloom like flowers bold,
While folks argue over the gold.
Surfboards stacked, a wobbly mess,
Everyone claiming they're the best.

Sandy snacks get lost anew,
As seagulls plot a heist, it's true.
Golden sands may calm the heart,
But beach towels do play their part.

Even the sun seems to chuckle,
Watching all the tourists wrestle.
In the shadow, chilled drinks clink,
Life's too fun, don't even think!

Echoes of a Warm Breeze

Whispers dance through palm fronds high,
Carrying tales of the sky.
Flip-flop symphonies in sync,
With giggles that make you rethink.

Sun hats flying, a comical sight,
Chasing after all that's light.
Surfboards surf on sandy dreams,
While sunscreen drips and laughter beams.

Feisty crabs with sideways glee,
Plotting mischief by the sea.
Pineapples wearing silly hats,
Laugh at sunburned kitty chats.

Even the waves seem to laugh,
As they splash on the crowded path.
In this land where giggles flow,
Joy is the best treasure to show!

Tropical Whispers Through the Canopy

Monkeys gossip high on trees,
Chattering like busy bees.
They pass secrets with a swing,
While birds join in to sing.

Lizards lounge on warm, flat rocks,
Wearing smiles like fancy socks.
They sunbathe without a care,
While ants march, unaware.

A parrot drops a fruit so round,
It bounces on the sandy ground.
With a squawk and a funny dance,
It seems to take a silly chance.

Frogs croak jokes beneath the shade,
Making laughter in the glade.
They ribbit tales of grand delight,
In every splash, joy takes flight.

Blossoms Beneath the Radiant Sun

Flowers giggle in the breeze,
Pointing out the buzzing bees.
With colors bright and scents so sweet,
They dance along to nature's beat.

A butterfly with polka dots,
Winks at bumblebees in plots.
Together they throw a wild bash,
In a whirl of colorful flash.

Vines twist like dancers in a row,
Whispering secrets, low and slow.
Palm trees sway, donning a grin,
As tropical fun is about to begin.

Beneath the sun's warm embrace,
Laughter brightens every space.
Nature shares its joyous glee,
In petals and giggles, wild and free.

Sunlit Journeys Through Lush Terrain

A tortoise plods in slow parade,
While crickets sing, their fun displayed.
With each step a giggle ensues,
As it searches for its favorite muse.

The monkeys swing from branch to branch,
Playing tag—a daring dance.
They tumble down with silly grace,
Not a worry on their face.

In the distance, a hammock sways,
Promising naps on lazy days.
But instead, a parrot swings by,
With feathery jokes, oh my oh my!

A quick race with a chubby mole,
Who's lost in thought, that's the goal.
Laughing out in the bright terrain,
In this wild world, joy won't wane.

Dreams Woven in Tropical Colors

A painter comes to find his muse,
In every flower, a different hue.
Mangoes grin, and coconuts giggle,
As the palette breaks into a wiggle.

Dancing waves wear sparkly shells,
While crabs tell tales of oceanbells.
Each wave a brushstroke on the sand,
Creating art, quite unplanned.

With laughter rising with the tide,
Clouds drift softly, oh what a ride!
A splash of fun in a sunlit dream,
Nature's canvas is a gleam.

So gather here beneath the trees,
Where every moment brings you ease.
In colors bright and whimsies grand,
Life's funny tale we'll understand.

Nature's Temple of Light

Sunshine spills like lemonade,
On leaves that go for a parade.
Lizards dance, with tails that sway,
While bees hum tunes, on their sweet ballet.

A squirrel hops in a silly way,
Chasing shadows, in leafy play.
Coconuts fall with a thud,
As birds laugh, picking seeds from the mud.

Frogs croak jokes in the afternoon,
While crickets strum their own monsoon.
A monkey swings, oh what a sight,
Falling once, but brimming with delight.

A Symphony of Tropical Serenades

In the jungle, laughter flies,
With parrot squawks and firefly sighs.
The wind plays tricks, a cheeky tease,
As palm fronds rustle, dancing with ease.

A turtle tries to join the race,
He's not first, but finds his pace.
Giggling toucans on the branch,
Chant a tune, a colorful dance.

A sloth picks leaves, oh so slow,
While ants march past, putting on a show.
With every chirp and funny flair,
Nature's party is beyond compare.

Cultivating Warmth Within

Warmth nestles deep in the soil,
Seeds sprout stories—no need to toil.
Cactus wears a smile so bright,
While big sunflowers bask in light.

Bananas giggle on their vine,
Whispering secrets, oh so fine.
Lemons laugh in zesty cheer,
As oranges bounce, "We're all here!"

Every fruit a tale to share,
And plants hold laughter in the air.
A garden filled with glee and fun,
Warms the heart like morning sun.

Together Under the Mango Tree

Gathered 'neath the mango's shade,
We swap our jokes, unafraid.
Children giggle, running wild,
As shadows dance, every child.

The mangoes are both ripe and bold,
Their sweetness, a treasure to hold.
With each brave bite, we share delight,
As laughter rises, soaring high as flight.

A picnic spread on a leafy floor,
With chatter loud, who could want more?
Under canopy, we toast the day,
With mango juice in a fun array.

Dances of the Tropical Breeze

Palm trees sway with a giggle,
Beneath the sun's warm wiggle.
Laughter bubbles in the air,
As crabs try to dance with flair.

Tropical fruits join the show,
Mangoes putting on a glow.
Coconuts roll with a cheer,
While toucans shout, 'Over here!'

The sun plays peek-a-boo,
Sipping on its morning brew.
Frogs croak in silly tones,
As friends trade their funny bones.

A breeze whispers a mishap,
Napping on a straw hat nap.
It lifts and sends it flying,
While everyone else starts crying.

Radiance Over Coral Reefs

Underwater disco party starts,
Fish parade with goofy arts.
Corals blush with laughter's hue,
As bubbles pop like giggling dew.

An octopus twirls with grace,
While seahorses pick up the pace.
Clownfish swim in funny rows,
Pretending to strike silly poses.

Starfish rock out on the floor,
Doing moves you can't ignore.
A turtle tries breakdance moves,
While jellies glide in smooth grooves.

Echoes of the ocean tease,
As laughter rides the gentle breeze.
Under the sun, all's a blast,
Splashing fun, we'll make it last!

Catching Sunbeams in Paradise

Sunbeams play tag on the sand,
As flip-flops fly, a goofy band.
Seagulls squawk their silly tune,
Searching for snacks 'neath the moon.

Kids jump high, with wild cheer,
Chasing shadows that disappear.
A sandcastle's leaning, oh dear!
But crabs just laugh without fear.

Beach balls bounce with great might,
While sunscreen makes a slippery sight.
Friends race waves with squeals of glee,
Falling, they plunge like a big tree!

At sunset, droplets of gold,
Paint stories of fun to be told.
With a grin and a wink, we say,
Let's catch more sunbeams every day!

Vibrant Echoes of Nature's Canvas

A parrot squawks in vibrant hues,
As monkeys swing like they've got shoes.
Flowers bloom with a chuckle near,
Their petals giggle when we cheer.

Butterflies flit with fancy grace,
Donning spots of a colorful face.
Grasshoppers jump in silly ballet,
While frogs croon a tune, come what may.

Caterpillars waddle with pride,
While fireflies join in for the ride.
Under stars that twinkle and play,
Nature's canvas brightens the day.

As night falls, the crickets sing,
A symphony of funny bling.
With each note, we laugh and spin,
In this dreamy world, let's dive in!

Fireside Stories in Paradise

Around the fire, we tell our tales,
Of singing fish and giant snails.
The marshmallows roast, the laughter flies,
As we share our dreams beneath starry skies.

A parrot squawks, it steals my hat,
It thinks it's funny, I think, 'How brat!'
We dance like crabs, we sing like fools,
In this silly circus, we break all the rules.

The moonlight glimmers on the sea,
A jellyfish floats just to tease me.
Coconut drinks spill on my chest,
In this comedy, I am the jest!

We tell ghost stories, then burst with glee,
The shadows dance, oh, can you see?
With every laugh, we forget the world,
In this paradise, our joy unfurled.

The Journey Toward the Horizon

We hopped on a boat, with snacks galore,
Our captain said, 'Let's explore!'
But where we headed, who could know,
With jellybeans guiding, we went with the flow.

A dolphin waved, with a grin so wide,
'Come swim with us!' it said, full of pride.
But we just flailed, like noodles went,
Splashing the sea, what a funny event!

The sun dipped low, like a big warm pie,
We sang to the clouds, daring them to cry.
But they just chuckled, and so did we,
As a seagull swooped down, pesky and free.

With each new wave, our spirits soared,
Adventure awaits, we can't be bored.
For in this journey, so wild and bright,
We found joy and laughter, from day into night.

Beneath the Golden Canopy

Under palm fronds, we share our snacks,
A monkey peeked, perhaps it attacks!
We all laughed hard, a raucous cheer,
As it grabbed a chip and disappeared.

The sunbeams danced, a golden show,
On our sunburned backs, we felt the glow.
But sunscreen mishaps led to some burns,
And laughter erupted as the tide churns.

We played peek-a-boo with ladybugs,
Laughter like music, sweet warm hugs.
The avocado toast, a brunch delight,
Got swiped by seagulls, taking flight!

With each mischief, our spirits lifted,
In this vibrant world, we felt so gifted.
Beneath the canopy, our hearts were free,
In silly moments, we just had to be.

Sunlit Shores and Whispering Palms

The beach was packed, with toes in sand,
We built a castle, oh so grand!
But waves snuck in, with a cheeky sneak,
And laughed as our fortress turned to leak.

Shells crunched underfoot, a real delight,
'Is that a dog or a seal in sight?'
We squinted hard, our brains in a spin,
Till a kid with a frisbee made us all grin.

The sun blazed down, so bold, so bright,
We chased imaginary aliens, what a sight!
Slipping on ice cream, a classic fall,
We rolled in the sand, giggling through it all.

As palm trees danced, in the gentle breeze,
We found ourselves laughing, just with ease.
With every wave and every call,
Our joy lit up like a beachside ball.

Dancing Through Sun-Kissed Vistas

Beneath the sun, we prance and whirl,
With visions bright, we laugh and twirl.
The palm trees nod, they join our spree,
In this warm realm, we're wild and free.

Sandy toes and cheeky grins,
Competitions of who spins wins.
Seagulls watch with keen delight,
As we jig about, a joyful sight.

Stray dogs join in, with wagging tails,
They dance along, ignoring gales.
We trip and slip, it's all a game,
In sunny bliss, we feel no shame.

With sun hats huge and drinks so cold,
Our laughter echoes, brave and bold.
This is our world, a curious stage,
Where every footstep writes a page.

Kaleidoscope of Nature's Palette

Bright blooms pop, like paint on a brush,
A rainbow of laughs in every hush.
The bees are buzzing, oh so spry,
They dance too, beneath the sky!

Butterflies flit with style and glee,
Wearing colors that make us see.
We try to catch them, take a selfie too,
But they just laugh, as if they knew!

The grass tickles our legs in delight,
As we chase shadows, frolic in light.
Playing hide and seek with the breeze,
Nature's giggles put us at ease.

Each petal's wink brings cheer to our hearts,
With every bloom, a new smile starts.
We're part of this canvas, wild and bright,
Turning each moment into pure delight.

Embracing the Spirit of Tropical Wildflowers

Among the blooms, we weave and sway,
A parade of colors, a joyous display.
The daisies chuckle, the orchids grin,
As we frolic about, with silly spin.

The scent of nectar fills the air,
With butterflies giving us a stare.
Ducks quack tune, the frogs join the song,
In floral kingdom, we all belong.

Pineapples mock with their spiky hats,
While bananas swing like playful bats.
We twirl with joy at nature's place,
Where flowers laugh and none keep pace.

The sun dips low, the laughter rolls,
With every petal, we chase our souls.
In this garden, so blissfully bright,
We dance till dusk, in pure delight.

Chasing Sunrays on Golden Sands

The beach is calling, let's have some fun,
With sun-kissed faces, we're second to none.
We play tag with waves, ride our own high,
While sandcastles grow, reaching for the sky!

Shells scatter around like treasures untold,
Each one a story, as we strike gold.
Seashells giggle, as we pile them high,
Making crowns fit for a king with a sigh.

Seagulls swoop, with cries like banter,
They're stealing snacks like a cheeky dancer.
While sunburns creep, we dive into cool,
Talentless flips, we make it a rule!

So here we lay, with laughter and cheer,
In this golden realm, all we're missing is beer.
As waves kiss our toes, we let out a cheer,
In this sandy wonderland, we hold dear.

The Allure of Golden Tropic Nights

Palms sway, dancers in the breeze,
A monkey swings with charming ease.
Stars peek through, a wink and a grin,
While crabs conduct a hasty spin.

Coconut drinks, so sweet and cold,
With tales of treasures yet untold.
A parrot squawks, a comedian's boast,
While lizards play at being the host.

The ocean hums a playful tune,
As fireflies join the midnight moon.
A party forms on sandy shores,
Where laughter echoes, and fun restores.

Glimmers of joy in every glance,
Even the fish seem to dance!
The tropics sing a vibrant song,
Where silly moments truly belong.

Stillness in the Glow of Twilight

The sun dips low, a golden show,
While crickets chirp, their evening glow.
A sloth dangles from a nearby tree,
Critiquing all with utmost glee.

Bats flit about, with grace and flair,
Chasing their shadows without a care.
An iguana strikes a curious pose,
As though he's lost all sense of prose.

A sudden splash? What was that sound?
A fish leaps high, but not quite round.
The night air hums, the laughter flows,
While mischief hides where the soft wind blows.

In the twilight's embrace, chaos reigns,
In every heart, a joy remains.
A moment etched in time, so bright,
As nature chuckles in the night.

Serenade of the Sunlit Wilderness

A monkey's shout breaks through the haze,
As butterflies join the joyful praise.
The sun peeks in, a golden laugh,
While ants march off in a wobbly path.

Lizards sunbathe, plotting their schemes,
While tourists snap their hopeful dreams.
Cicadas chirp their buzzing refrain,
As laughter floats on a playful train.

Palm trees sway, a dance so grand,
While beaches offer a warm, soft hand.
The waves join in, a rhythmic beat,
Where every misstep feels like a treat.

With nature's quirks and surprises around,
The wilderness sings, enchantingly loud.
In sunlight's embrace, we find our song,
A serenade where we all belong.

Reflections of Joy in Tropical Solitude

A hammock sways, my thoughts take flight,
As seagulls perform a silly fight.
The ocean mirrors my whims and dreams,
Where fun and folly dance in beams.

A coconut falls with a comical thud,
As I sip joy from a vibrant bud.
The sun sets low, painting skies in gold,
While crabs strut by, feeling quite bold.

Time slows down in this silly place,
As I lose myself in nature's embrace.
The laughter echoes, the joy expands,
In these quiet moments, life truly stands.

With every wave, a chuckle or two,
The solitude sings of something new.
In the calm, I find my vibrant call,
A giggle shared by one and all.

Shadows Beneath the Mangroves

Amidst the roots, a crab does dance,
While iguanas steal a fleeting glance.
The sun is hot, but so are we,
In this green world, wild and free.

A lizard slips, a splash! Oh no!
Into the water, with quite the show.
The laughter echoes, the day goes on,
In muddy shoes, we'll sing our song.

Mangoes drop from trees above,
While parrots squawk of endless love.
All while we sip on coconut juice,
To life's tropical, silly use.

Come join the fun, leave dull behind,
Beneath the shade, new joys we find.
The mangroves whisper secrets sweet,
What a funny way to beat the heat!

The Call of Tropical Birds

A parrot squawks, it sounds like me,
With tales of nuts and cups of tea.
The toucan's honk is quite a gaff,
Makes every creature start to laugh.

From high above, the eagles dive,
While pigeons strut like they're alive.
Fowl chatter fills the humid air,
Who knew a bird could have such flair?

Each chirp and tweet, a story shared,
"Oh look, it's lunch!" one bird declared.
A feast of fruit, so bright, so grand,
Their silly antics across the land.

We dance to the songs of feathered cheer,
With laughter ringing far and near.
For in the tropic's vibrant song,
We find the humor all along.

Serenity in Solitude

Alone I sit, with laughter near,
A coconut falls, oh dear, oh dear!
The waves just giggle, tickling my toes,
While the sun sets, and the breeze blows.

The crabs do waltz in the golden sand,
With funny moves, by nature planned.
A hermit's house is but a shell,
"I'd trade it for a condo, well, well, well!"

Reflections dance upon the glass,
As I laugh at thoughts of grass.
For solitude hides a joyful jest,
In every wave, I find my rest.

With flip-flops off, my heart takes flight,
In the whisper of dusk, I feel so light.
Peaceful moments, we chuckle and weave,
In this paradise, oh how we believe!

Dancing Shadows at Dusk

When daylight fades, the shadows grow,
They stretch and yawn, starting the show.
The monkeys swing, a comic delight,
With whoops and hollers, they take flight.

The palm trees sway, a sultry dance,
As fireflies join in the fanciful prance.
A crab joins in, with moves so grand,
It's a hidden talent, not quite planned.

Each flickering light tells tales of mirth,
In the softening glow, there's magic and earth.
Giggles erupt from the forest's heart,
Dusk's gentle whispers playfully start.

So let us twirl under the starry view,
Where shadows dance, and all's brand new.
In this warm embrace of the tropic's dusk,
We find our joy, a little must!

Vibrant Flora and Fauna

The parrot screams a morning tune,
As lemurs dance beneath the moon.
The iguana shows off bright green flair,
While turtles take a slow, cool glare.

A frog hops by, a yellow spot,
Sipping juice, he's quite the lot.
With flowers blooming everywhere,
Even bees just cannot care.

The monkey swings from tree to tree,
Stealing fruit – oh, what a spree!
And in the garden, ants parade,
While nature laughs, unafraid.

So here's to life in colors bright,
Where laughter bubbles, day and night.
With critters playing, flowers sway,
Let's join the fun, come what may!

Dappled Sunlight on Sand

On golden grains, flip-flops fly,
As sand crabs scurry, oh my, oh my!
A beach ball bounces, kids all shout,
While sunscreen's slathered without a doubt.

Seagulls swoop with zealous zeal,
Stealing fries – that's quite the meal!
A surfboard wobbles as riders fuss,
While jellyfish float with no rush.

Umbrellas painted like rainbows bold,
While stories of mermaids are told.
The sunbeams dance in playful spins,
As laughter echoes and merriment wins.

So grab a drink and chill some more,
This sunny spot is not a bore.
With salty breezes and cheeky laughs,
Let's savor our tropical gaffs!

The Rhythm of Ocean Waves

The ocean hums a silly song,
As surfers paddle, trying to belong.
Waves crash loud, but don't you fret,
The fish just swim, no need to sweat.

A dolphin jumps with such delight,
While crabs play tag, oh, what a sight!
The tide rolls in, a foamy dance,
As sandcastles wobble, no second chance.

The seals all bark, holding court,
As sunbathers vie for best spot.
And jellyfish drift like melted dreams,
In this surfside land of silly schemes.

So ride the waves or watch the show,
Join in the fun, don't be too slow.
For in these tides, both wild and free,
Laughter flows, just like the sea!

Colors of a Caribbean Dawn

With dawn's first light, the skies ignite,
As roosters crow with all their might.
A splash of pink, a dash of gold,
While sleepyheads dream on, untold.

Lemons dance in morning breeze,
As coconuts sway with careless ease.
The sun peeks in, a warm embrace,
And sleepy critters find their pace.

Coffee brews with fragrant cheer,
As breakfast plans draw ever near.
Bacon sizzles, eggs abound,
With laughter rising, all around.

So rise and shine to greet the day,
In this vibrant land, come what may.
With colors bright and laughter loud,
Let's celebrate, be joyful and proud!

The Golden Embrace of Dusk

The sun yawns wide, a sleepy glare,
Lizards dance without a care.
Coconuts chuckle on swaying trees,
While parrots gossip in the evening breeze.

As clouds wear orange coats so bright,
Crickets tune up for their night flight.
A dog in the distance tries to sing,
But it's just an off-key thing.

The breeze flips pages of lazy days,
As fireflies join the twilight's plays.
Beneath the stars, the night awakes,
While everyone hears the giggle of lakes.

So toast to the dusk, a golden treat,
With laughter echoing, life's a feat.
In warm embrace, we'll spin and sway,
As the moon rolls in to steal the day.

Enchantment of the Sunlit Isles

On shores where the sun pours like sweet tea,
Even the crabs are dancing with glee.
A parrot cracks jokes that only she gets,
While iguanas curse their missed sunbaths bets.

Sea turtles glide, slow as my aunt,
Who swims like she just learned to chant.
Waves tease the rocks with playful splashes,
While locals sip drinks of fruity fashes.

The palm fronds wave like they're at a show,
As sunbathers compete in the who-can-snooze-faster flow.

Seagulls bring snacks, or maybe they try,
To steal my sandwich, oh my, oh my!

So let's frolic on sands of golden hue,
And let laughter be our daily brew.
In this island world, fun never fades,
As sunshine dances and silliness parades.

Emerald Shadows and Golden Hues

Under emerald leaves, shadows play,
Where monkeys swing in the silliest way.
A breeze whispers secrets, but don't take a note,
For it's probably tripping on an old boat.

The flowers burst forth, a colorful crew,
Chasing the sunlight, turning bright blue.
While lizards wear shades, feeling quite cool,
And the chameleons ponder, "Am I a fool?"

The waves crash laughter, frothy and wild,
As children chase dreams, the sunlight's a child.
Giggles echo while palm fronds sway,
In this paradise, we'll frolic and play.

So let's twirl in shadows, swim in the beams,
With laughter that lingers and bright sunny dreams.
In shadows and colors, our hearts will unite,
As we bask in this joy, day turns to night.

Traces of Dawn on Tropical Shores

As dawn breaks gently with a sleepy yawn,
The world pours honey with a golden dawn.
Crabs crawl sideways, keeping it cool,
While seagulls play lifeguard, acting the fool.

The salty air whispers morning pranks,
As the sun paints stripes on the ocean banks.
Sandy toes wiggle, tickling tales,
While palm trees sway, telling tall gales.

A fisherman fumbles, his net turns confetti,
While the sunrise chuckles, oh isn't that petty?
With bright-colored boats lined like a parade,
They bob and they wave, mischief displayed.

So here in the morning, where giggles align,
With the laughter of waves, the true grand design.
Let's dance on the shores, chase the light's tease,
In this paradise, our hearts find their ease.

Secrets of the Rainforest

In a jungle thick with green,
The monkeys swing like they're on a scene.
Parrots squawk with vibrant flair,
While ants march, without a care.

Sloths hang out, just taking naps,
While snakes do sneaky little laps.
The trees gossip, leaf to leaf,
About the sloths' slow belief.

Bugs dance wildly, what a show,
While frogs croak tunes that steal the flow.
The sun peeks in, a sly old cat,
As every creature wears a hat.

With laughter echoing through the shade,
Nature's antics never fade.
In this lively green parade,
The fun and folly never trade.

Reflections of an Endless Horizon

Under the sun's cheeky grin,
Waves crash down with a splashy spin.
The crabs scuttle, looking for dinner,
While seagulls argue who's the winner.

Sandy toes and sunburned nose,
Beach volleyball? Everyone knows.
Tanned tourists with ice cream cones,
Melting quickly, turning into drones.

Kites flutter like laughing flies,
While kids build castles, oh so wise.
But waves come in, with sneaky might,
Turning towers into a soggy sight.

As the day fades into night,
Bug spray dances in the twilight.
With memories of that endless play,
We leave the shore, but wish to stay.

The Embrace of Humidity

The air is thick like peanut butter,
With a humidity that makes you stutter.
Sweaty brows and sunburned cheeks,
In this heat, nobody speaks.

The mister fans whirr like bees,
Trying hard to please, please, please.
The breeze has left, gone on a trip,
As we sip lemonade with a lip.

Grasshoppers jump with electric might,
But we just stick to our chairs tight.
The flip-flops flop, what a sound,
As we lounge around, quite unbound.

Yet in this sticky, funny plight,
We find our joy, our pure delight.
For laughter in the sultry air,
Turns humidity into a funny affair.

Moonlit Nocturne by the Shore

The moon winks like a cheeky sprite,
As waves giggle in the night.
Stars twinkle with a playful tease,
While owls hoot, trying to please.

Driftwood dances in the sand,
As shadows play in the moonlight band.
Crickets serenade the cooling breeze,
While night creatures hum their melodies.

Tide pools sparkle, holding a show,
Reflecting laughter as they flow.
A jellyfish glows, a silly sight,
Drifting around in soft twilight.

With each splash, we jump and cheer,
Under the moon, there's nothing to fear.
As the night unfolds its gentle spell,
We embrace the magic, time will tell.

Ocean's Embrace in a Sea of Sunlight

The waves dance like a startled fish,
A seagull dribbles, making a swish.
Sandy toes tickle with each frothy crest,
While sunburned backs take a much-needed rest.

Beach balls bounce, oh what a sight,
Umbrellas tilt to dodge that bright light.
Crabs in their shells do the moonwalk too,
While I'm stuck in a flip-flop, what to do?

Flickers of Joy in Paradise

Coconuts giggle from palm trees tall,
The hammock sways like a funhouse hall.
Laughter echoes like a mischievous breeze,
As sunscreen wars unfold with ease.

Fish in the bay wear sunglasses so cool,
While dolphins jump, breaking the rule.
The sunset blushes, the sky takes a bow,
And I just spilled my drink all over my brow.

The Heartbeat of the Tropic Lands

Tiki torches flicker, a party awaits,
While I trip on my flip-flops, oh the fates!
A parrot squawks jokes from his branch so high,
As I dance like a fool, laughing 'til I cry.

Mangoes drop like confetti from trees,
Sticky smiles bloom in the warm, sweet breeze.
Sunsets bring shimmer, but listen, my friend,
I'm wearing my sunglasses- it's how I pretend!

Cadence of the Sunlit Waves

A ukulele strums, a tune so fine,
While beachgoers wobble in a dance line.
Seashells gossip, they whisper and giggle,
As the waves crash with an oceanic wiggle.

In flip-flops I stumble on soft, golden sand,
While crabs throw their hands up, it's all unplanned.
The tide rolls in, with a cheeky grin,
Life's a lighthearted spin, let the laughter begin!

Golden Hours and Coral Dreams

Sunrise shakes the sleepy trees,
Coconuts dance in the warm breeze.
Flip-flops squeak on sandy trails,
Laughter echoes like happy whales.

Beach balls roll like runaway dogs,
Sunburned noses chase after frogs.
A parrot squawks a silly tune,
While kids build castles beneath the moon.

Watermelons chilled by the sea,
Seagulls eyeing treats just for me.
Tropical hats flop in the sun,
Sipping coconut drinks, oh what fun!

With every wave, the giggles rise,
Shells shimmer under bright blue skies.
Life is a carnival down here,
Where every moment brings us cheer.

Infusion of Sun and Sea

Surfboards wobble, catch the breeze,
Sandy toes and sticky knees.
A crab declares, "This is my patch!"
While we laugh and watch it hatch.

Tanned tourists slip on ice-cream,
Melting drips—not quite the dream.
Beach towels flutter, flags on high,
Even starfish attempt to fly!

A hammock sways as naps unfold,
Marking tales of legends told.
The sun dips low, a fiery friend,
Disco ball of light won't end.

Ice-cold drinks are slurped with glee,
While dolphins dance in jubilee.
Every sunset starts a tale,
In this juggle of sun and sail.

Footprints on Sunlit Shores

Tiny footprints zigzag around,
Seagulls squawk, their joy unbound.
With shovels digging to the core,
We wonder what's in store!

A beach ball bounces, slips, and flies,
Chasing giggles, beneath warm skies.
The tide comes in, we make a dash,
Splashed by waves in a watery splash!

Sunscreen chaos on every face,
Sticky fingers in a sweet embrace.
Sandcastles crumble with every wave,
Learning lessons—we must be brave!

Under palm trees, we set our base,
Share silly tales that time can't erase.
The shoreline glows, a perfect quest,
Where laughter reigns and hearts find rest.

Sunlit Reverie of Ocean Breezes

A sun hat flies with the breeze,
Chasing after warm, playful bees.
Beachcombers searching for a prize,
Find seashells shaped like little pies.

Tiki torches spark as night falls,
While laughter echoes through the halls.
Toasted marshmallows, sticky bites,
Roasted under starry nights.

Waving flags in a bright parade,
A crab and seagull, grand charade.
Frolicking waves dance on the sand,
With every giggle, life is grand!

Skimming stones, we take our aim,
Splashing water like a game.
Oh what a day, we'll sing and dream,
To make memories, our ultimate theme.

www.ingramcontent.com/pod-product-compliance
Lightning Source LLC
Chambersburg PA
CBHW072217070526
44585CB00015B/1372